Stepping Up to Google Classroom

50 Steps for Beginners to GET STARTED

Alice Keeler and Kimberly Mattina

This book is available at special discounts when purchased in quantity for use educational purposes or as premiums, promotions, or fundraisers. For inquiries and details, contact the publisher at books@daveburgessconsulting.com.

Published by Dave Burgess Consulting, Inc.
San Diego, CA
DaveBurgessConsulting.com

Paperback ISBN: 978-1-951600-14-3
Ebook ISBN: 978-1-951600-15-0
Library of Congress Control Number: 2020935493

Cover and interior design by Liz Schreiter

Contents

Introduction

This book is not the ultimate guide to Google Classroom. In fact, an experienced Classroom user will probably notice that several features aren't covered at all. This was intentional. Why? Because *Stepping Up to Google Classroom* was specifically created for educators who are new to Google Classroom and looking for a way to get started. We wanted this book to be a step-by-step guide for beginners, not an exhaustive resource.

One of our favorite phrases is *paperless is not a pedagogy*, and we've used that principle to guide our approach for beginners to Google Classroom. So this book does get you started using Google's powerful online education tools, but it's also designed to help you go beyond a merely paperless approach to education. Rather, the goal is to improve student engagement and learning.

Without that mission, the research is clear, just using new technology will not improve engagement, nor will it create meaningful gains. In fact it's the opposite! Several studies show students perform *worse* when we switch to a digital environment.

When making the transition to Google Classroom, it is incredibly important that we really stop and reflect before simply putting things online. We must look at which research-proven practices actually improve student learning.

Remember, too, the fact that you are new to Google Classroom means that your assignments were designed for paper. Paper is not bad! If an activity was designed for paper, use paper! Besides, kids should do something besides interact with a screen all day.

What all this means is that while it might seem like your obvious first step with Google Classroom should be to do something like making electronic copies of documents for your students, we encourage you to start your journey by considering how you can use this tool to interact with those students.

Like any digital tool, Google Classroom requires a different approach. But while we have to design for the medium, we must still consider the four Cs—critical thinking, communication, collaboration, and creativity—and aim to include at least one of them in each activity we create.

> *"One of the things a teacher can do is stop administering low-level worksheet activities and empower students to produce representations of their knowledge even if they contain errors and omissions! Learning is an iterative process not a one-and-done process!"*
>
> —Sonny Magana

Collaboration is fundamental to Google Classroom, so it becomes a natural consideration when designing lessons. Communication can look like so much more than students just answering a question, and going beyond text with Google Classroom provides many exciting formats for students to clearly communicate their ideas. Creative thinking means not every student has to submit the same thing, and Google Classroom makes it easy to leave an assignment open-ended enough to result in a diversity of end products. It's a great tool for critical thinking, too. Critical thinking can be measured by the Depth of Knowledge (DOK) level on a four-point scale. Worksheets and book work gener-

ally operate at the DOK 1 level, requiring recall and reproduction. When a Google search is at our students' fingertips, we might wonder how to stop them from looking up the answers to the questions on those worksheets—instead, we must realize that we have to change the questions. Designing for the medium of Classroom means increasing the critical-thinking demands of tasks so that access to a Google search is not "cheating."

So paperless is not a pedagogy, but shifting to using digital education tools can allow you to change how you teach, and that change *can* improve learning!

Visit 50thingsbook.com for a tour of Google Classroom

Stepping Up to Google Classroom

1. Access Google Classroom

Access Google Classroom by going to **classroom.google.com**.

The first time you go to Google Classroom, you will be asked if you are a teacher or a student. It is essential that you select **I'm a Teacher**. Users designated as **Teachers** can enroll as a student in a class in addition to being able to teach a class. Those designated as **Students** can enroll in a class or co-teach a class. If you accidentally choose **I'm a Student**, contact your school's G Suite administrator to address the issue.

Google Classroom's home page is called **Classes**, and it displays tiles for the classes that you teach or are enrolled in as a student. Each tile will list the class title, section, how many students are enrolled, and any assignments—with due dates—that are upcoming in the next week

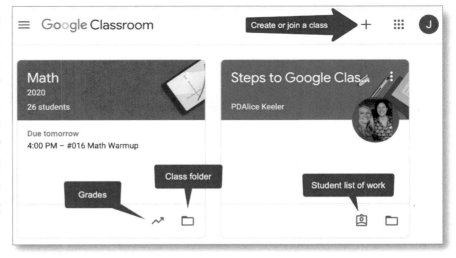

> ### Google Classroom Tip
> Create a new class every six weeks or for a new unit, semester, or marking period. This makes it easier to reuse assignments for a new class. You can archive classes from the class tiles by clicking on the **Three Dots**. Assignments can still be reused even if the class is archived.

2. Create a Class

You must be designated as a **Teacher** to create a class.

In the upper-right corner of Google Classroom you will find a **Plus Icon**. Click on this icon and choose **Create Class**.

> ### Google Classroom Tip
> Take advantage of the **Section** line when creating a new class. We recommend that you include the school year and your name.

3. View the Stream

After creating a class, you will be immediately taken to its **Stream**. The **Stream** is the landing page for your class, and it's a great quick reference for teachers and students to access announcements and assignments.

The **Stream's** header will display a default image, and you'll likely want to change the picture there. In the bottom-right corner of the header image, you can click on **Select Theme** to choose a new theme from the **Gallery**.

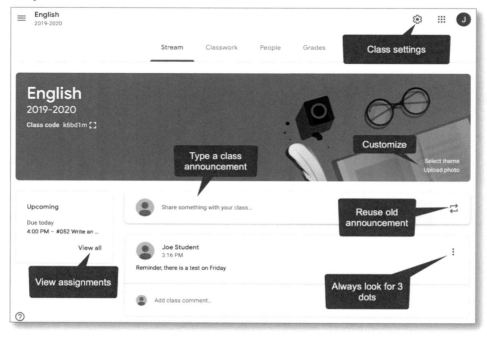

> ### Google Classroom Tip
>
> Create your own custom header for your Google Classroom. Try making one with the Google Drawings template at **alicekeeler.com/gcheader**. When you're done, use the **File** menu to **Download as PNG** for upload into Google Classroom.

4. Go to the Settings Cog

In the upper-right corner of Google Classroom is the **Settings Cog**. This opens an area where you can review and change the course details and general settings for things like student permissions to post and comment to the **Stream Page**, how classwork attachments for posts are shown, and **Grading**.

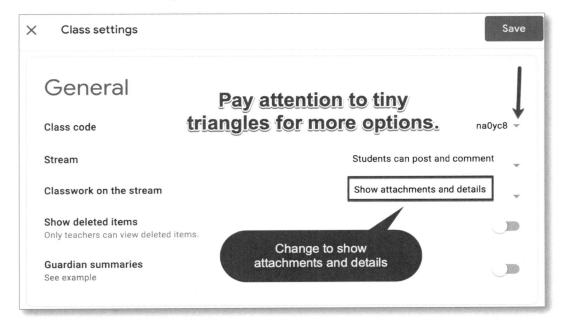

In Google Classroom you can always click on the **Tiny Triangles** for more options.

> ### Google Classroom Tip
>
> It is important that students of all ages and grades, including kindergartners, are able to join a Google Classroom class using the **Class Code**. In the **Settings**, use the **Tiny Triangle** next to the **Class Code** to reset the code. Reset the **Class Code** until you are positive that no student will inadvertently type the code incorrectly. To avoid problems, try not to use the letters "O" or "I" or the numbers "0" or "1," which can easily be confused for each other. Once the code is set, you can come back later to use the **Tiny Triangle** to display the code to allow students to join your class.

We highly recommend that you leave **Students Can Post and Comment** set to **on**. Google Classroom is an opportunity for you to teach students how to behave and interact online. Expect that students will make immature choices on what they post to the **Stream**, but know that this is not a reason to turn off the feature, but the opposite. When students post immature or inappropriate things, they are demonstrating a need for students to be taught how to appropriately post online. Expect that they will not learn the first time.

> ### Google Classroom Tip
>
> Making it easier to see attachments and details helps students get to work more quickly. Class comments on an assignment are only visible on the **Stream** when **Show Attachments and Details** is selected. As a teacher, this option allows you to see quickly if students have submitted work so you can interact more quickly with students.

Whenever you post an assignment to Google Classroom, it is announced in the **Stream**. By default, the assignment will appear as a condensed stripe with only its title. We recommend that you change the assignment-display setting—which appears as **Classwork on the Stream** in the **General** section of the settings menu—to **Show Attachments and Details**. This allows students to see an assignment's details without clicking and to more easily make a class comment from the **Stream**.

Note that you only need to enable **Show Deleted Items** after you delete inappropriate student comments and want to review the comments later with the student and/or another adult.

5. Set Grading Categories

The **Settings Cog** also allows you to set up the gradebook for Classroom. The grading capabilities of Google Classroom are very rudimentary. Leave **Overall Grade Calculation** and **Show Overall Grade to Students** set to **off**.

On the **Assignment Stripe**, Google Classroom shows grading categories for every assignment. Set up the categories that you want displayed to the students. A default point value for each category is required.

> ### Google Classroom Tip
>
> Instead of grading categories, consider using assignment types. This helps students clearly identify what type of activity they are completing. Suggestions for assignment types include: Warm-Up, Exit Ticket, Mastery Quiz, Independent Practice, Project, Group Work, Class Discussion, and Test.

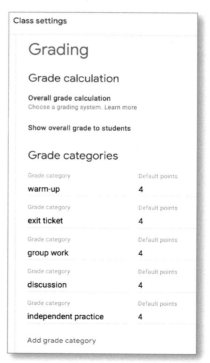

6. Create and Plan Out Topics

At the top center of Google Classroom, you'll find tabs for different pages. The most important page, **Class-work**, is where assignments are organized by topics and posted.

The **Classwork Page** is designed to be organized using topics. Plan out your topics by clicking on the **Create Button** on the **Classwork Page** and choosing **Topic**.

Planning out your topics allows you to think out and organize your **Classwork Page** without revealing the topics or drafted assignments to students until you're ready. Each topic will appear as a section on the **Class-work Page**. While organizing the topics by units might seem like the most logical approach, do not feel con-strained by that format. You may instead want to orga-nize your topics by week, day, or activity type.

> **Google Classroom Tip**
>
> Use the header image to help direct students to the **Classwork Page**. Use the template at **alicekeeler.com/goto** to create a Classroom header with a finger directing students to click on the **Classwork Page**.

> **Google Classroom Tip**
>
> Topics without active assignments posted are invisible to students. This allows you to plan out units in advance without revealing topics and assign-ments to students.

The older the information, the lower it should appear on the **Classwork Page**. You want students to log in and, with minimal scrolling, be able to see what work they need to do. When planning out your topics, you might also want to consider the information students see first. If organizing topics by unit, plan out the unit topics in reverse order.

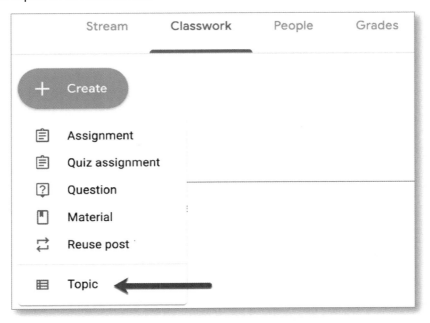

We suggest a list of topics like the following:

- Respond to Feedback
- Today
- About/Resources
- Unit 5
- Unit 4
- Unit 3
- Unit 2
- Unit 1

An order like the following is another good option:

- Respond to Feedback
- Today
- About/Resources
- Unit Resources
- Challenges
- In the News
- Week 3
- Week 2
- Week 1

Topics and assignments can be dragged to reorganize the **Classwork Page**. Once topics are created, you can always drag and drop them into the desired order.

> **Google Classroom Tip**
>
> Actionable feedback is highly effective for learning. Often, students will hyper-focus on a score and all but ignore your feedback. For that reason, we recommend not releasing students' scores until they respond to your feedback. Create a **Respond to Feedback** topic at the very top of the **Classwork Page** so that students are aware of which assignments you have provided feedback and that they need to address that feedback. Once all of the students have responded to your feedback, you can drag the assignment to the topic it should be organized under.

7. Get Your Files into Google Drive

Files in Google Classroom are managed by Google Drive. When you upload a file to Google Classroom, it is not stored in Classroom; instead, it's actually uploaded to Google Drive from Google Classroom. The uploaded file is then linked into the assignment from Drive. The file is shared with the students.

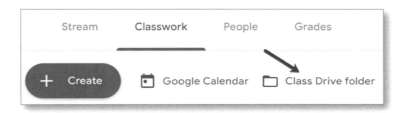

We suggest that you get all of your files and resources into Google Drive directly. Or, better yet, create all of them using Google Apps, like Google Sheets, Google Docs, or Google Slides. Creating all of your resources with Google Apps will make it much easier to integrate them with Google Classroom.

> **Google Classroom Tip**
>
> Your **Class Drive Folder** is *your* folder. Students do not have access to it, so saving files to the folder does not share them with students. Open the **Class Drive Folder** (found on the **Classwork Page)** to find the assignment folders and student work.

8. Review the Create Button

To add items to the **Classwork Page**, use the **Create Button** at the top of **Classwork**. The first option is to create an assignment, which is the option you will use 90 percent of the time. In Google Classroom, assignments are anything you want students to interact with. Assignments can be designated as ungraded, which can be useful if they are meant to be resources for students or in-class activities.

Clicking on **Quiz Assignment** creates a Google Form for you with preset quiz options. You may want to skip this option and simply create a Google Form yourself and then add the Form to an assignment. Creating the Google Form directly will give you more control over how the quiz is set up.

> **Google Classroom Tip**
>
> Visit **forms.google.com** to create a Google Forms quiz.

When we ask a question and students raise their hands to answer, we only end up hearing from a few of them. But the ability for a teacher to hear from *every* student is powerful for learning. Using the **Create Button** for a **Question** will make an assignment that allows you to poll the class with either a short-answer or multiple-choice question and allow every student to participate.

The **Materials** option allows you to add view-only resources or links.

Save time by using the **Reuse Post** option to re-use an assignment that was previously posted to another current class or an archived class.

> **Google Classroom Tip**
>
> Unlike assignments, the **Materials** option doesn't allow for class discussion or for students asking private questions. That's why you might instead consider creating an ungraded assignment for resources, which does allow for interaction around the material.

9. Add a Class Resources Topic

You will need your own topic (named something like "about" or "resources") on the **Classwork Page** to post materials such as a class syllabus, textbook link, class website link, etc. These are simply resources you wish to share with your students, not necessarily assignments. Use either an ungraded assignment or the **Materials** option from the **Create Button** for these resources.

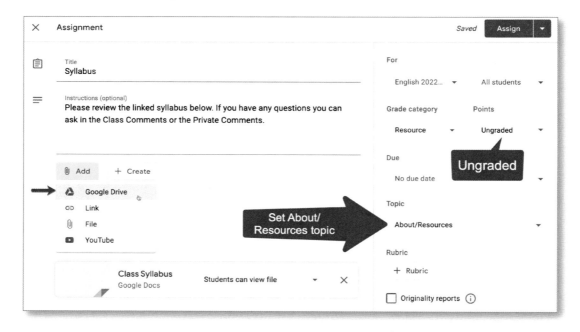

> **Google Classroom Tip**
>
> You may want to use an "about" or "resources" topic to separate new material students are working on from past assignments. Make the current unit the top topic, and follow it with the "about" topic and then previous units at the bottom.

Use the **Add Button** to upload files from your computer, add a file from Google Drive, link to a You-Tube video, or link to a website.

> ### *Google Classroom Tip*
> Since all files in Google Classroom are actu-ally links to Google Drive, you can update your resources directly in Google Drive. This allows you to be sure that the resources are updated for all classes that utilize them.

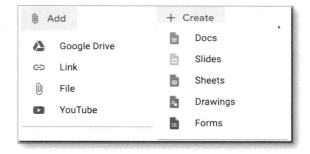

10. Number Your Titles

When we talk less, students can do more. Numbering everything you put into Google Classroom with a hashtag and three-digit number, such as #001, allows you to use less words when directing students to something in Google Classroom.

Every assignment has a "question 1," so using the hashtag in the title number distinguishes "Assign-ment #001" from "question 1" in any document you have in your Google Drive. Searching Google Drive or Gmail for the hashtag and three digits will be quicker because only the assignments you're looking for will appear in the results.

Even younger students benefit from assignments being numbered. Though their reading ability might be limited, they are capable of matching. Write the assignment number on the board to al-low students to recognize what assignment they need to open.

> ### *Google Classroom Tip*
> Don't start your assignment-numbering scheme over when you create a new class at the start of the grading period, unit, or semester. Instead, continue the numbering or start from a new number. There should be only one "Assignment #004" for the entire school year.

> ### *Google Classroom Tip*
> Elementary teachers may want to consider assigning each subject a separate number-ing scheme. For example, you could use 100s for math and 200s for science.

11. Ask a Question

Using Google Classroom is not about just throwing all of your stuff online. It is a mindset for interact-ing with students.

One of the easiest ways to start interacting online is to use the **Question** option under the **Create Button**. When you do that, use the first line to ask the question. Below that, you can provide more details on what you are looking for from students' responses.

The default question type is **Short Answer**. Always be on the lookout in Google Classroom for **Tiny Triangles** to give you more options. Next to the **Short Answer** designation, click on the **Tiny Triangle** to change the question to multiple choice. Note that students will be required to respond to the question before they are able to see responses from other students.

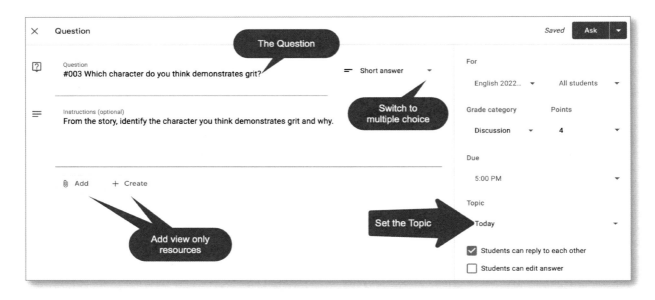

Google Classroom Tip

Questions are designed for peer feedback. When asking for a short-answer response, we highly recommend you leave **Students Can Reply to Each Other** set to **on**.

In a typical class, when we ask a question we only hear from the same handful of students. Asking a question digitally allows all students to actively participate. Google Classroom also aids in providing sufficient wait time to allow students to answer. As students submit their responses, a count appears showing how many have been received and how many are yet to come.

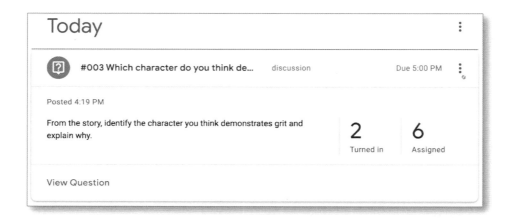

> ### Google Classroom Tip
>
> Make a habit of adding questions to Google Classroom spontaneously. When creating assignments, occasionally skip the option to choose a topic. This will post the assignment at the top of the **Classwork Page** so students can find it easily. Later, drag the question to the desired topic on the **Classwork Page**.

12. Create a Nondigital Assignment

Trying to jump into the deep end and go paperless can be confusing and make the transition to Google Classroom more difficult. Instead, focus on interacting with students as your first step.

Posting nondigital assignments to Classroom helps you to get used to utilizing a digital platform without becoming overwhelmed with its features. (A nondigital assignment is anything you do in class that does not require technology, like, for example, answering questions from a book on paper.) Always consider how an activity makes learning better, regardless of whether it's digital or not. No matter the format of the assignment, Google Classroom allows for improved interactions, conversations, and feedback.

> ### Google Classroom Tip
>
> When you post all of your assignments to Classroom—digital or nondigital—you provide students a single reference they can use to find out everything happening in class, and because they can ask digitally, students are more likely to ask questions. Since every assignment allows for a private comment, Classroom instantly makes every assignment interactive.

Post all assignments into Google Classroom with a directions document to create a more student-centered classroom where students get more work done. That way, students won't have to wait for verbal instructions when they walk into class. Instead, they can access Google Classroom and follow the directions they find there, even when an assignment does not have to be completed digitally. Putting the directions in Classroom allows you to talk less and better use your time to support students.

In the assignment, click the **Add Button** to link to your directions document from Google Drive or click the **Create Button** to start a fresh directions document.

Remember to pay attention to the **Tiny Triangles** when posting an assignment:

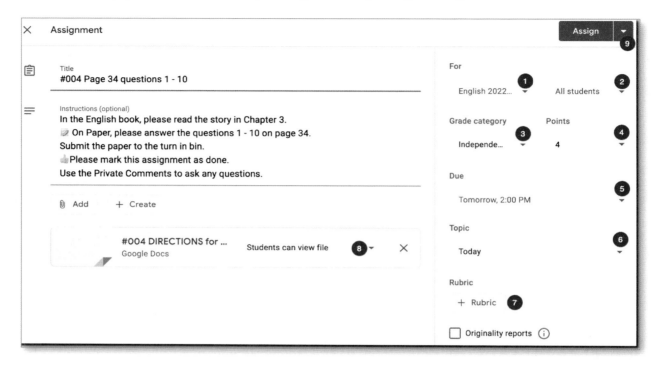

(1) Select multiple classes

(2) Assign to selected students

(3) Set grade category

(4) Change the point value

(5) Set a due date

(6) Assign a topic

(7) Add a rubric

(8) File distribution

(9) Schedule the assignment

Clicking on the **Assign Button** will immediately make the assignment visible and available to students. For students who have email enabled, an email notification with a link to the assignment will be sent. Students will also see the assignment announced on the **Stream**.

Google Classroom Tip

Create a short video or screencast in which you explain the directions and expectations for an assignment. The Screencastify Chrome extension is a great tool for easily creating these videos, which are then conveniently saved to Google Drive. Your Google for Education account has unlimited storage in Google Drive, and adding videos to Classroom from Google Drive avoids some of the pitfalls of utilizing YouTube. Learn how to use Screencastify from Matt Miller in his free one-hour certification course at **screencastify.com/master**.

13. Create an Assignment for Multiple Classes

Google Classroom allows teachers to post the same assignment to multiple classes at one time. This is a huge time saver! To do this, simply create an assignment, provide the assignment details, and click on the small triangle next to the class name in the side panel. A drop-down list displaying all of your classes will appear. Simply check the box next to the classes for which the assignment is relevant, then hit the **Assign Button** to post the assignment to the **Classwork Page** for all of the selected classes.

Note that If you need to make a change to an assignment, you'll have to modify the assignment in each of the classes separately.

> ### *Google Classroom Tip*
> Some elementary teachers will organize different subjects, such as math and reading, into separate Google Classroom classes.

14. Assign to Selected Students

Google Classroom makes differentiation easier.

Notice that the default audience when creating any assignment is **All Students**. Click on the **Tiny Triangle** next to **All Students** to select or deselect assigned students. Deselected students will *not* see that the assignment exists; it will only appear for the students explicitly assigned.

> ### *Google Classroom Tip*
> To ensure that students with modified assignments do not feel singled out, after selecting a subgroup of students to receive an assignment, use the **Reuse Post** option from the **Create Button** at the top. Reuse the assignment you just created, assign it to a different subgroup of students, and modify the instructions. The assignments' numbers will be identical, but the directions will be modified. Each student's **Stream** looks the same, but the instructions do not.

15. Explore the Three Lines Menu

Find the **Three Lines Icon** in the upper-left corner. This indicates a menu. Click on the **Three Lines** to open a sidebar.

The first option there, the **Home Icon**, will return you to the **Classes Page**. You can switch to a different class by choosing its tile on the **Classes Page**, or you can switch between classes directly from the sidebar menu. At the bottom of the **Three Lines** menu, you can access the settings and your archived classes. The **Settings Cog** in this side menu will allow you to manage your Classroom notifications, change your profile picture, and manage notifications for a particular class.

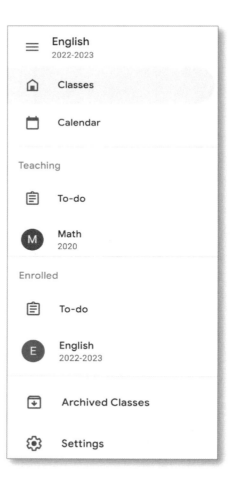

> ### *Google Classroom Tip*
> You can rearrange the class tiles on the **Classes Page** by either dragging the tiles or by clicking on the **Three Vertical Dots** on a tile and then opting to **Move** that class. Rearranging classes on the **Classes Page** also rearranges the order of the classes in the **Three lines** menu.

16. Post an Announcement

The **Stream Page** is where you can begin a conversation with your students.

Navigate back to the **Stream** by clicking on the class title in the upper left or by clicking on the **Three Lines** menu in the upper left. You can type an announcement to the **Stream** in the dialogue box immediately under the banner. Start by welcoming students to the class and inviting them to click on the **Classwork Tab** to find a question you've left for them.

Students can continue discussions among themselves beyond the school day. The **Stream** allows students to express their opinions about a topic in a constructive manner. The **Stream** can also be used by teachers to post daily learning goals, daily agendas, or encouraging messages to students.

> ### *Google Classroom Tip*
> When assignments are announced to the **Stream,** they will push down older announcements. Clicking on the **Three Dots** on the announcement allows you to **Move to Top** to bring it back to your students' attention.

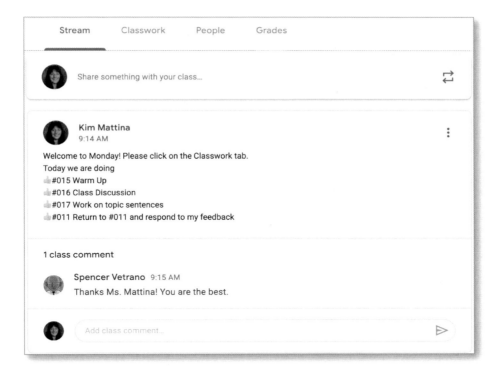

17. Display the Class Code

Now that you have your Classroom settings configured and some assignments ready for students to interact with, it's time to add students to your class.

You can easily view the **Class Code** in the header on the **Stream**. Next to the code is a **Broken Square Icon** that allows you to display the code for students. Alternately, you can click on the **Settings Cog** to access the code in the **General** section, where you can choose **Display**.

Display the **Class Code** and direct students to **classroom.google.com**. Clicking on the **Plus Icon** in the upper-right corner allows students to type the join code for your class. This instantly takes them to the **Stream**. From there, students can get started on the activities you have left for them in Google Classroom.

While you can invite students to your Google Classroom via email, we recommend sharing the **Class Code** with them instead. You might need to make a small investment of time to teach them how to join Google Classroom, but the return is great: students will not only learn how to join a Classroom for themselves but they'll get to exercise their agency as independent learners.

18. Discuss Digital Etiquette and Classroom Expectations

Social media and digital interactions are elements of our modern world that are not going away any time soon. It is essential that we teach students how to behave properly and politely online because these are not natural skills. The Google Classroom **Stream** is an opportunity to teach students about social media and appropriate posting.

Ask students to share a post on the **Stream** like one they'd put on Instagram or Facebook. This is an excellent way to learn more about your students, to build relationships, and to teach. Students will respond in immature ways. Again, this is not a reason that they should be muted but rather evidence that they need opportunities to try social digital interactions and to receive instruction on how to be kind social citizens.

We highly recommend going over digital etiquette and digital citizenship with your students by using Google's Be Internet Awesome and Interland. Interland teaches students about online safety and digital citizenship in a fun and engaging way in a gaming environment. It also offers a pledge and a free curriculum that you can download and integrate into your classroom. You can visit **beinternetawesome.withgoogle.com** for information about both resources.

> ### *Google Classroom Tip*
> Building relationships is one of the most important things we do as teachers. Not only does using the **Stream** as a social media platform allow us to teach students how to behave in the real world, which includes social media, it also gives us insights to who they are as people.

Another great resource is Common Sense Media. This website has a ton of materials that reference online safety. Visit **commonsensemedia.org** for more information.

19. Students Mark as Done

Upon viewing any assignment, students will find a **Your Work Bubble** in the upper-right corner. Students can **Mark as Done** to indicate they have participated in or completed a task. They can add documents, pictures, or links to the assignment submission in the **Your Work Bubble**. Adding files changes the button's verbiage to **Turn In**.

> ### *Google Classroom Tip*
>
> Every assignment allows students to ask a private question. Students are more likely to ask a question if they can ask it digitally. Encourage students to reflect on the assignment or ask a question in the private comments when they submit an assignment.

Students should use **Mark as Done** for nondigital activities. This helps both you and the students keep track of all classroom activities. Teachers can use private comments to leave digital feedback on any activity.

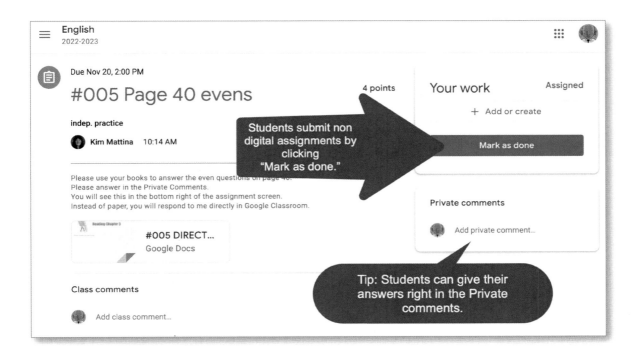

20. Return to the Classwork Page

After they **Mark as Done**, students will need to return to the **Classwork Page** for the next assignment. Clicking on the class title in the upper-left corner will return the student to the **Stream**. This allows them to see if there have been any class announcements, peer questions, or new assignments posted since they started the assignment. Students need to be directed to return to the **Classwork Page** by clicking on **Classwork** along the top.

> ***Google Classroom Tip***
>
> Show students a shortcut for opening an assignment: They can hold down the **Ctrl** or **Shift** keys when they click on **View Assignment** to open the assignment in a new tab or a new window without leaving the **Classwork Page**. Closing the tab returns the student to where they were on the **Classwork Page**.

21. Students Create Their Own Documents

Instead of linking a Google Apps file to an assignment, allow students to create a file with the Google App of their choice within the assignment. When students use the **Add or Create Button**, they will have the option to create a document, presentation, drawing, or spreadsheet file that is automatically linked to the assignment. Students can access these files through the assignment or through Google Drive.

As soon as a student creates a file within the assignment, it's instantly shared with the teacher. This gives you immediate access to the file and allows you to monitor their work and provide critical feedback while the student is still working on the assignment.

Assignments with student work automatically create a subfolder in the class folder in Google Drive. This folder organizes all of the documents the students create for a particular assignment.

> ***Google Classroom Tip***
>
> Reduce "autopsy feedback." We get the highest return on feedback when we leave it for students before they think they are done with an assignment. As often as is reasonable, access student work before the due date to provide students guidance on their work. As Robert Marzano highlights, students need to be given feedback while there is still time to improve.

22. Students Add Additional Files

When students are ready to submit an assignment, they have the option to include additional resources to support their work. These can include anything in their Google Drive, links to third-party applications, or other files stored on their devices.

This option is important because it allows students to think outside of the box, display their tech savviness, and develop the ability to support their work independently. It also supports student choice and creativity.

> **Google Classroom Tip**
>
> Allow students to create screencasts to record and explain their work. The Screencastify Chrome extension works on Chromebooks to allow students to record their screen and explain or present their work. The screencast file will automatically be saved to a Screencastify folder within the student's Google Drive. Students can easily add their screencast to an assignment by clicking on the **Add Button** or **Create Button** and selecting the **Google Drive Icon**. Check out the Screencastify Jr. certification with Holly Clark for your students at **screencastify.com/jr**.

23. Students Turn In Work

When students include files in an assignment, they will see a **Turn In Button**. When a student presses **Turn In**, you are notified that they are done with their work and it is ready to be assessed. It also changes the student's status from **Assigned** to **Turned In**. You can see a count of the number of students who have **Turned In** an assignment by clicking on the **Assignment Stripe** on the **Classwork Page**.

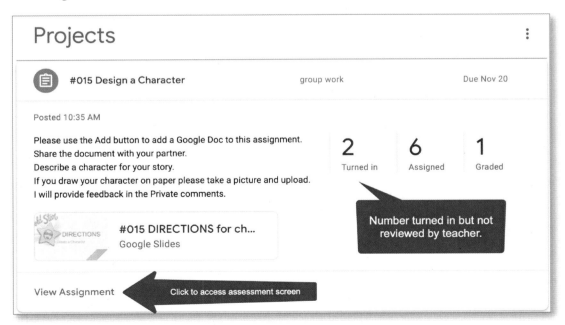

> **Google Classroom Tip**
>
> We recommend that you go to the **Settings Cog** and enable **Show Attachments and Details** under the general settings. When you do, you can easily see which assignments have work to be graded from the **Stream Page**. This is significant because in Classroom it's no longer necessary to have all students submit their learning at the same time. With that constraint gone, when one or a handful of students have turned in the assignment, you're free to provide feedback.

"There is no average time to learn something."

—Dr. Thomas Guskey

Keep in mind that when students turn in work, they lose editing rights and become viewers of their documents. You become the owner of the document until you return the work.

> **Google Classroom Tip**
>
> If students turn in work after the due date, you will receive an email notification of late work submitted. Filtering your Gmail for **Late Submitted** allows you to go through the "late pile."

24. Locating Student Work

If you have enabled **Show Attachments and Details** in the **Settings Cog**, you will be able to scroll the **Stream** to find the count of students who have turned in work. Click on the number for **Turned In** to open the **Assessment Screen**.

> **Google Classroom Tip**
>
> Use the **Google Drive Folder Icon** under the **Turned In** count to quickly see all student documents. Use the sorting and filtering options in Drive to see who last modified their document so that you can provide feedback faster.

You can also access the **Assessment Screen** from the **Classwork Page** by clicking on any **Assignment Title** to expand it. This will show the count of how many students have turned in a given assignment. From there, click on **View Assignment** or **View Question** to open the **Assessment Screen**.

On the left-hand side of the **Assessment Screen** is a roster of the students in your class. The students who have turned in the assignment will be listed first, followed by students who have not. For any student, click on their name to review their work.

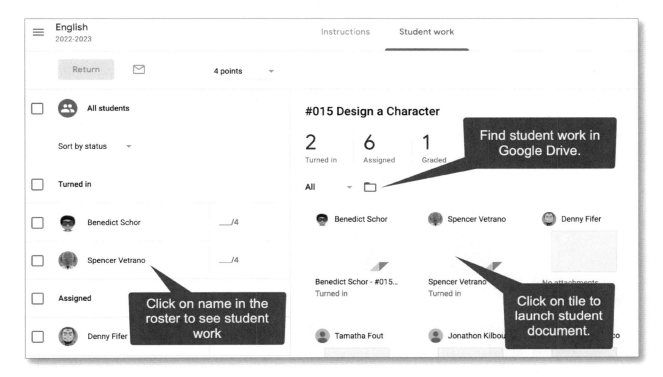

25. Use the Feedback Tool

Accessing student work from the **Assessment Screen** will open it in the **Feedback Tool**. The **Feedback Tool** is a frame around the document that allows you to review the student's work and leave comments in Google Classroom.

For Google Text Documents, the default is **Suggestion Mode**. This enables you to suggest edits directly in a student's paper. You can switch from **Suggestion Mode** to **Editing Mode** in the **Feedback Tool**.

> **Google Classroom Tip**
>
> Use the keyboard shortcut **Ctrl-Alt-M** to insert comments to the side of the student's Google Doc, Sheets, or Slides. **Ctrl-Enter** will save the comment.

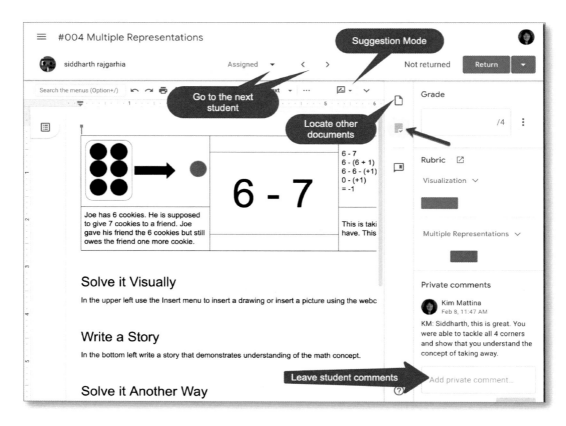

Notice the two icons on the sidebar of the **Feedback Tool**. The top one allows you to toggle between student documents, if more than one has been submitted for a given assignment, and to leave feedback or utilize the **Assignment Rubric**. The bottom icon opens a **Comment Bank** that you can populate to make leaving feedback faster.

Close the tab of the **Feedback Tool** to return to Google Classroom.

26. Leave Assignment Feedback with Private Comments

Every assignment created in Google Classroom allows for private comments, which are confidential between the teacher and student.

In the **Assessment Screen**, click on a student name in the roster on the left-hand side. Then, on the bottom right, you will see an option to add private comments.

> ### Google Classroom Tip
> On the roster to the left side of the **Assessment Screen,** you can see a comment preview. When leaving a private comment start the comment with your initials. The initials allow you to quickly identify comments that are yours, so you can click on student comments in the preview that still need a reply.

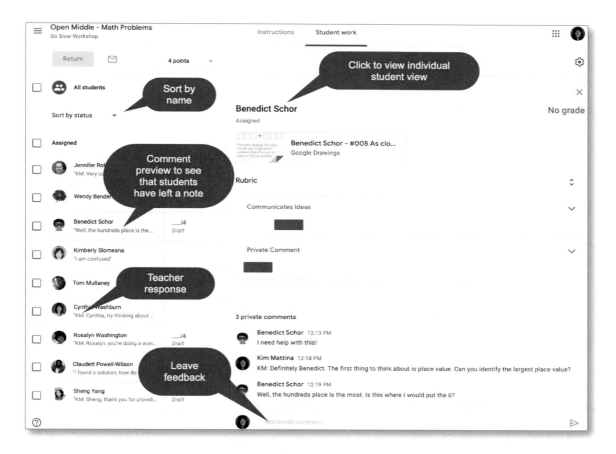

Students will receive an email notification when you leave a private comment. If email is not enabled for students, they can go to the **View Your Work Button** on the **Classwork Page**, which will display a **Comment Icon** next to any assignment that includes a private comment.

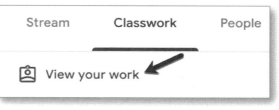

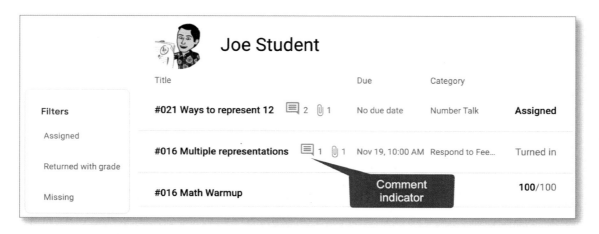

> ### *Google Classroom Tip*
> Leave students video feedback by using the Chrome extension Screencastify. Clicking the extension will allow you to choose your webcam and record your face and/or screen. The video is automatically saved to Google Drive. Click the option to copy the link. Paste the link (**Ctrl-V**) to leave video feedback in the private comments.

27. Announce when Feedback Is Given

For students to review and respond to your feedback, they have to know that you have left it. If you give feedback and a student never sees it, you've wasted your time.

As previously mentioned, when you leave feedback, students will receive an email notification and an indication that private comments are available on the **View Your Work Page**, but we recommend that you more explicitly direct students to your feedback.

To do this, click on the **Three Dots Icon** on the **Assignment Stripe** and choose the option to **Copy Link.** Create a new announcement on the **Stream** to indicate you have left feedback on the assignment and provide the link right in the announcement.

> ### *Google Classroom Tip*
> After students have made steps in response to your feedback, have them describe in the private comments what updates they made and resubmit the assignment.

Edit

Delete

Copy link

Move up

Move down

28. Assign a Private Comments Exit Ticket

Try using a private-comments-style assignment as an exit ticket. From the **Classwork Page**, use the **Create Button** to choose **Assignment**. In the description, ask students an exit ticket question and prompt them to respond in the private comments.

This gives you time to reply to each student individually in the private comments. The next morning, the bell ringer is to respond to the comments you left them.

> ### *Google Classroom Tip*
> Conversations are more powerful than comments when it comes to learning. Uniquely, Google Classroom allows you to go beyond a comment and interact with students back and forth using private comments. Ask students to respond in the private comments instead of within a Google Doc to help facilitate better conversations.

29. Assign a Score

If an assignment is graded, you can leave students a score on the left-hand side of the **Assessment Screen**. The score is not visible to the student until the assignment is returned.

Google Classroom Tip

We recommend using rubric scores instead of assignment points to indicate assignment completeness:

0: Excused

1: Mostly incomplete. Needs major work done on it. Revisions required.

2: Needs significant improvement. Revisions required. Please respond to feedback given.

3: Needs minor improvements. Feedback suggestions given that you can optionally respond to.

4: Work is acceptable. No revisions required.

Google Classroom allows you to add a rubric to assignments to quickly give feedback in reference to predefined criteria. We recommend you turn off **Scoring** in the rubric to maintain the rubric as a feedback tool.

30. Return Student Work

Returning work is an important part of the Google Classroom workflow. Students will not see any points or in-document feedback until work has been returned. After providing feedback to students, you can return work from the **Assessment Screen** by selecting the checkbox next to a student's name and clicking the **Return Button** in the upper-left corner.

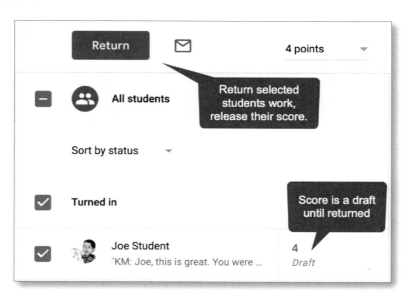

Returning work also changes the assignment's status. Students can find the status of an assignment by checking the **View Your Work Page**. When assigned, the status of an assignment is **Assigned**. If you included a due date, the status will automatically change to **Missing** if a student doesn't turn in work before the due date. When students submit work, the status becomes **Turned In**. Returning work with a score indicates to the student that you have reviewed their work. Their status is now **Graded**. For ungraded work, the status changes from **Turned In** to a green checkmark.

> **Google Classroom Tip**
>
> It is important to emphasize that when students submit work with documents to Google Classroom, the student is changed from owner of the document to viewer. Viewers cannot view in-document comments nor can they make edits or respond to edit requests until the assignment is returned. Be sure to return documents quickly to allow students to take action on your feedback.

> **Google Classroom Tip**
>
> Returning work without a score reassigns work to a student. Their status will change from **Turned In** back to **Assigned**. If you return work without a score after the due date, the status will be **Missing**.

31. Return to the Stream

In the upper-left corner of the screen is the class title. Clicking on the title will bring you back to the **Stream**. Review the **Stream** to see if any students have asked questions about the class and click back on **Classwork** to add an assignment or review an assignment.

> **Google Classroom Tip**
>
> In Google Chrome, navigate to the **Classwork Page**. Bookmark the page by clicking on the **Star Icon** in the **Omnibox** and saving the page to your bookmarks bar. This makes it faster to get to the **Classwork Page**.

32. Students Unsubmit Their Work

Sometimes, students realize that they forgot to include information in their Google App file after it has been submitted. Luckily, they have the option to unsubmit the assignment at any time. You can direct students to unsubmit their work by locating the assignment on the **Classwork Page** and clicking on **View Assignment**. From there, they will find an **Unsubmit Button,** which allows them to change the content of the file and resubmit it.

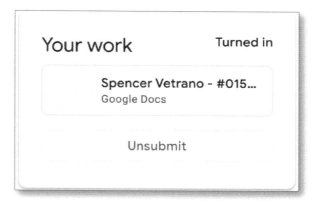

33. View Submission History

Technology allows us to rethink why we do things a certain way. In the past, teachers assigned work, students completed that work and handed it in to the teacher, teachers gave back graded work, and the class moved on to the next assignment. However, it's better for learning for teachers to provide students with actionable feedback and expect that they will respond to that feedback. With Google Classroom we can shift to a model of constant improvement.

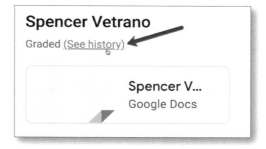

Within the **Assessment Screen**, find **See History** under a student's name.

The submission history shows the number of times a file has been turned in. This information can indicate if a student is struggling with an assignment. The teacher can provide additional support or reflect on the assignment description and revise it if necessary.

Spencer Vetrano's history

Returned: 4/4	1:59 PM	Kim Mattina
Draft grade: 4/4	1:59 PM	Kim Mattina
Turned in	1:59 PM	Spencer Vetrano
Unsubmitted	1:56 PM	Spencer Vetrano
Turned in	10:36 AM	Spencer Vetrano

Close

34. Link to Digital Quizzes

As we like to say, "If robots can grade it, they should." For low-critical-thinking questions, free yourself from the burden of grading by using tools that do the grading for you. These tools not only relieve you of the burden of grading low-critical-thinking questions, they provide students with immediate feedback, which will increase engagement and learning. Teaching students critical thinking is time consuming. Free up your time for providing high-quality feedback and guidance on higher-level activities.

From the **Classwork Page**, create an assignment and use the **Link Icon** to paste the link to a quiz you want students to complete. Ask students to reflect on the activity in the private comments.

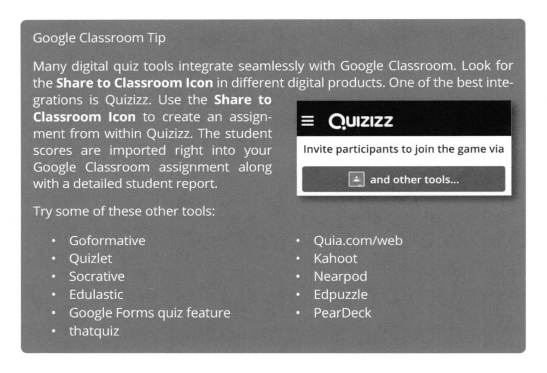

35. Have Students Submit Screenshots

Screenshots are not just an accountability tool. Yes, you can use them to be sure that students work on what they are supposed to be working on, but they also allow you to provide better support and feedback to students.

When using tools outside of Google, consider having students submit screenshots of work, progress, and final scores to Google Classroom. Students might be working on different activities or have personalized questions. For any assignment, students can click on **Add** to upload screenshots.

> **Google Classroom Tip**
>
> To take a screenshot on a Chromebook, students hold down **Ctrl-Shift-Windows Switcher Key**. The **Windows Switcher Key** is above the 6 key and looks like a rectangle with two lines to its right.

36. You Want Google Forms

Opening a separate document for every student and scrolling to where they entered answers on a line can be tedious and does not provide you any data.

Instead of uploading a Word document or using a Google text document as an assignment, you may want to use Google Forms to ask the same questions instead. As always, you can add Google Forms to any Google Classroom assignment by either using the **Add Button** and choosing the **Google Drive Icon** or clicking the **Create Button** to start a new Google Form from scratch.

> **Google Classroom Tip**
>
> If the only item you link to in an assignment is a Google Form, the assignment will automatically be marked as done when the student completes the Form.

Google Forms automatically creates a summary of responses, which allows you to more accurately and quickly determine what you need to reteach. On the responses tab in Forms, you can create a spreadsheet. Click on the green **Spreadsheet Icon** to view a copy of the responses in Google Sheets.

> **Google Classroom Tip**
>
> Try the Google Sheets add-on Flubaroo to grade Google Forms and provide specific feedback to questions. Feedback and reports can be emailed or sent to a document in Google Drive.

37. Try Quizlet Diagrams

> **Google Classroom Tip**
>
> Quizlet integrates with Google Classroom. Click on the swoopy arrow to assign a Quizlet directly to Google Classroom.

Consider how the student is getting feedback. Low-critical-thinking tasks should have immediate feedback.

Quizlet diagrams (**quizlet.com/features/diagrams**) not only allow students to receive immediate feedback, they also generate other activities to allow students to practice vocabulary in different ways. This is better for learning.

38. Check the To-Do List

In the upper-left corner of Google Classroom, you'll find the **Three Lines** menu, which provides you with a **To-Do List** for the classes you teach and are enrolled in.

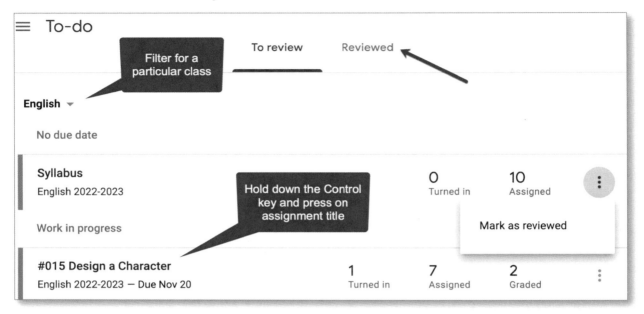

It is important to know if students have completed work so that you can respond quickly with feedback. By default, the **To-Do List** shows you a list of all your assignments for all of your classes. However, Google Classroom can show you a separate **To-Do List** for each of the classes you are teaching or enrolled in. Click on the **Tiny Triangle** to filter the list for only one class.

Remember, each **Assignment** shows the count of students whose statuses are **Turned In**, **Assigned**, or **Returned**. Click on the **Assignment Title**, the number **Turned In**, or the number **Assigned** to launch the **Assessment Screen**.

> **Google Classroom Tip**
> There is a hidden feature on the **Stream** for quickly accessing the **To-do Page** for just that class. Click on **View All** in the **Upcoming Bubble** on the left-hand side.

> **Google Classroom Tip**
> Hold down the **Ctrl** key when clicking on the **Assignment Title** to open the assignment in a new tab and not lose the **To-Do List**.

After reviewing an assignment, click on the **Three Dots** on the **Assignment** on the **To-Do Page** to **Mark as Reviewed**. This takes the Assignment off of your **To-Do List** so you can focus on work you're still actively providing feedback on.

39. Save an Assignment as a Draft

Plan out your assignments in advance and save them as drafts.

In order to save an assignment as a draft, click on the **Tiny Triangle** next to **Assign** and choose **Save Draft**. The draft assignment will appear grayed-out on your **Classwork Page**, but it won't be visible to students until you edit the assignment and assign it. You can further edit any assignment using the **Three Dots Icon** while it is in draft mode. You can not return an assignment to a draft state after it has been posted.

> **Google Classroom Tip**
>
> When co-teaching, always save your assignments as drafts. This allows your co-teacher to post the assignment and affords you both opportunities for collaboration.

40. Schedule an Assignment

Teachers can schedule an assignment to be posted to the **Classwork Page** on a specific date and time. This feature is useful when planning your assignments for the week or for a unit, and it is espe-cially helpful when you know you will be absent on a particu-lar day. All scheduled posts will appear organized by topics on the **Classwork Page**, and the icon associated with the as-signment will be grayed out.

> **Google Classroom Tip**
>
> Students receive notifications when assignments are posted. Schedule assignments for when class starts to avoid interrupting students while they're sleeping.

Use the **Tiny Triangle** on the **Assign Button** when creating an assignment to set the date and time for the assignment to appear in the class.

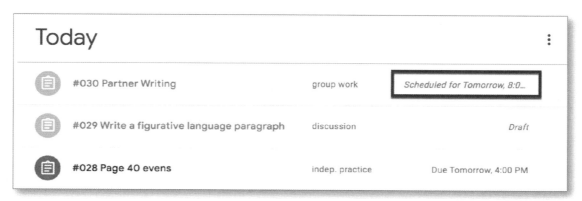

> ### Google Classroom Tip
>
> Assignments can only be scheduled for one class at a time. When you post an assignment to multiple classes, the scheduling option is grayed out. If you want to schedule the same assignment for multiple classes, first schedule it for one class. Then go into the **Classwork Page** for another class, click on the **Create Button**, and select the **Reuse Post** option. This will allow you to reuse the assignment posted to your other class and schedule it independently.

41. Reuse an Assignment from Another Class

Instead of working harder, we want to work smarter. Google Classroom has given us the ability to achieve this by providing the **Reuse Post** feature. This will allow you to copy a post from another class and add it to your current class.

> ### Google Classroom Tip
>
> You can reuse assignments from archived classes. When reusing a post you will select a class. Archived classes appear in the list of options for classes to reuse from.

To reuse an assignment from the **Classwork Page**, click on the **Create Button** and select **Reuse Post**. Find and select the class in the list, then find the post that you want to use in your current class. Once you've selected it, click on the **Reuse Button**. Now the post from the previous class will be shown in your current class.

> ### Google Classroom Tip
>
> When reusing assignments, you have the option to **Create New Copies of All Attachments**. Note that nothing is actually *attached* in Google Classroom. All attachments in a Google Classroom assignment are actually links to files stored in Google Drive. Making duplicate copies of the same documents creates a mess of your Google Drive and simply isn't necessary. So, always remember to uncheck the **Copy All Attachments** checkbox.

42. Collaborating in Classroom

Researchers like Robert Marzano and John Hattie agree on the value of cooperative tasks for benefiting learning. Students don't learn more because we upload documents; they learn more when we engage in cooperative tasks. Classroom and Google Apps are designed for collaboration.

When adding Google Apps documents to an assignment, click the **Tiny Triangle** to change from **Students Can View File** to **Students Can Edit File**.

Students can view file

Students can edit file

Make a copy for each student

Google Classroom Tip

Collaborating in a Google Doc works best when it is restricted to a small number of users. For more than three people, use Google Slides to collaborate instead.

You can easily add a collaborative Google Slides to any assignment. Click the **Create Button** within the edit screen and choose Google Slides. This will open a new blank Google Slides tab. In the upper left of the Slides document, change the title from "Untitled presentation" to the assignment number and approximately what you want the students to type on the slides. Back in the assignment, change the setting to **Students Can Edit Document** before assigning.

#029 Write a figurative language paragraph

File   Edit   View   Insert   Format   Slide   Arrange   Tools   Add-ons   Help

Google Classroom Tip

Collaboration is not a natural skill, digital or not. Students must learn it, so expect that it will take practice before all students get the hang of being on the same Google Slide.

Initially use the collaborative Google Slides activity as you would whiteboards to get students used to cooperating on the same document. Ask students to add a slide and put their name in the speaker notes. Each slide is like a blank piece of paper or a whiteboard. Move on to doing classwork collaboratively through Google Slides.

Google Classroom Tip

Make collaborative Google Slides a staple in your classroom. When work is done in a single Google Slides document it becomes easy to click the **Present Button** and generate class discussion and peer feedback around student work. Not only does this alleviate you of the burden of providing all the feedback, but students genuinely benefit more.

43. Use Version History

Working collaboratively means that sometimes we need to go back and review what a document looked like before a collaborator made changes.

To do this, use the File menu in Docs, Sheets, Slides, or Drawings to select **Version History** and then click **See Version History**.

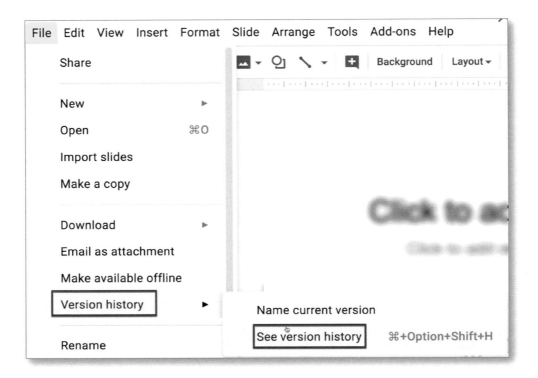

When a whole class works together on the same Google Slide, one student may inadvertently (or purposefully) delete the work of another student or make other undesired changes. Use the version history to restore the document to the way it was before.

> ### *Google Classroom Tip*
> When reviewing an individual student's work, use the **Pop Out Icon** from the **Feedback Tool** to view the document outside of the **Feedback Tool**. You can use the accompanying version history to see the work progress of a student. A lack of version edits can indicate that a student copied and pasted much of their work.

44. Students Submit the Link to Their Slides

Each slide in Google Slides has a unique URL. From the desktop browser (but not on mobile), students can copy the link to their own slide and paste it into the **Private Comments Bubble** in Google Classroom. Collaborating on the same Google Slides opens up many possibilities, including reduced paperwork for you. Students, however, can submit their individual work from the collaborative Google Slides by submitting their slide's link.

> ### Google Classroom Tip
> Students cannot submit work they do not own. They will be unable to use the **Link Icon** in Classroom to turn in their slide since you are the owner of the Slides. Instead, the student will need to paste the link into private comments.

45. Install the Google Classroom App

Google Classroom has an app for iPhones, Android phones, and iPads. Installing these apps gives you additional capabilities, along with the option to access student work or post assignments from anywhere.

> ### Google Classroom Tip
> Try opening assignments students are working on in class in your Google Classroom app on mobile or iPad. This displays a roster of student names. Tap on a student's name to leave private comments.

46. Create a Copy per Student

Remember, when using digital tools you are teaching differently. While you may be used to making photocopies for each student, interacting digitally with your students and using tools that grade digitally for you may be better options.

When adding documents from Google Drive to an assignment, you have the option to **Make a Copy for Each Student**. We recommend you choose this option on 20 percent or less of assignments because it can be equivalent to assigning yourself piles of digital paperwork, and it's not necessarily the best way to improve student learning.

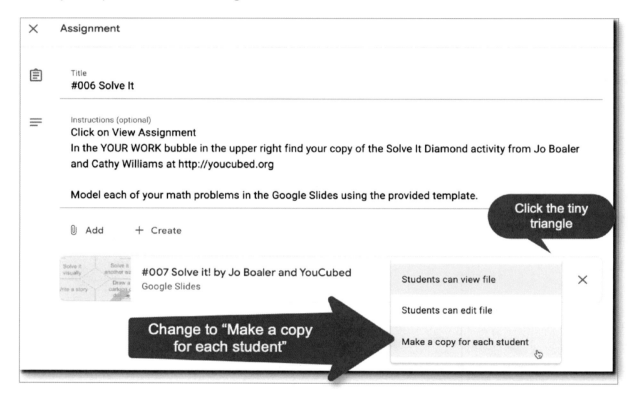

> ### Google Classroom Tip
> Reserve making copies for each student for larger projects that require ongoing feedback during the project process. When assigned critical-thinking activities, students will need actionable feedback to push their learning. Make comments in individual documents and leave a private comment letting students know they need to respond to the comments you left.

47. Use Google Slides

Constraints force creativity. Try to avoid assigning Google Text documents that you have to scroll through in favor of more creative options. Using Google Slides allows for a multimedia response from students. Slides also allows you to add a slide of your own to give students feedback rather than restricting you to side comments. You and your students are able to add video responses and feedback to the Slides document. When students use Google Slides over Google Docs, they have more creative options.

> **Google Classroom Tip**
>
> What can you not do on Google Slides? Slides are like a blank piece of paper. Like with Docs, you can comment on a specific word or phrase.

48. Create a Feedback Conversation

If you ask a random group of kids what percent of the work they are assigned is "busywork," you might be shocked. Some students seem to think that as much as three-quarters of their work isn't important to their learning. Kids think of assignments this way because they misunderstand their goals: they believe the point of turning work in is that they can be scored on it and then move on to the next assignment as quickly as possible. Of course, teachers have a very different perspective on this!

To ensure that learning—not the next assignment—is the result of student work, use tools like Google Classroom to have students enter into a conversation about the work with you.

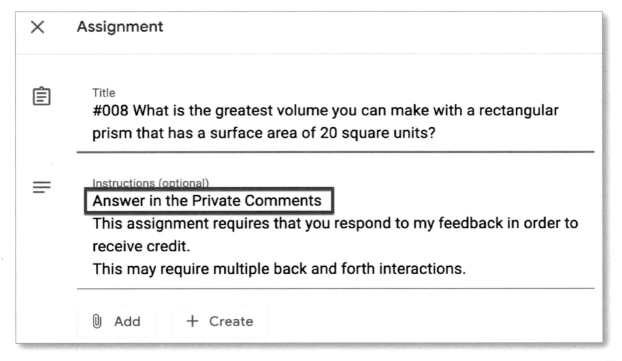

Return assignments without a score, and require students to use private comments to respond to your feedback. Release their scores only after they've engaged in a back-and-forth interaction with you and expressed what they've learned.

> **Google Classroom Tip**
>
> Success builds success, but you have to know your students to know how far you can push them in a feedback conversation before they get frustrated. Relationship building is essential. Some students will not provide as detailed a response as others, but do not compare one student to another. What does progress look like *for that student?* If the student made progress and responded to your feedback, it is imperative that you give *full credit*. This keeps the focus on the learning, and avoids responses like "See, I told you I couldn't do it" or "Why did I lose five points?"

49. Manage Email Notifications

Google Classroom generates a lot of email for you. These emails can be very helpful for alerting you to action in Google Classroom. However, they can also be overwhelming. We recommend that you do not disable email notifications but rather filter Gmail to allow you to review email notifications when you're ready.

Look at each of the emails sent from Classroom and notice the text that is repeated in subject lines for each type of notice. Filter for these emails and apply a Google Classroom label.

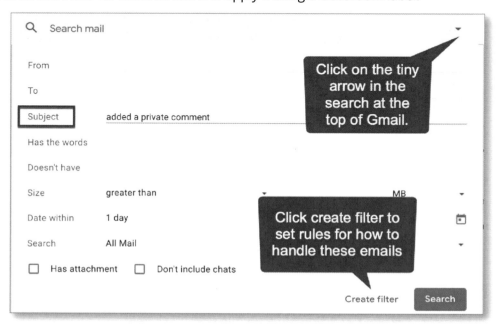

It is important to not miss private comments from students, since interacting with students is what we do best as teachers. So, create a filter for private comments and tackle these emails first.

> **Google Classroom Tip**
>
> After reviewing alerts from Classroom, delete the emails. There is no reason to save them. All of the information is in Classroom.

50. Add a Co-Teacher

If you are team teaching, it may be necessary to invite a co-teacher to your Google Classroom. The co-teacher will be able to access the Classroom. However, there are some minor things you should pay attention to.

First, the primary teacher is the only person who can delete the class. Second, the primary teacher cannot be unenrolled or removed from the class. Third, the primary teacher owns the Google Drive Classroom folder, even though the co-teacher will have access to it.

To invite a co-teacher, simply go to the **People Page**, and click on the **Add Person Icon** at the top-right side in the teacher section of the page. Next, type the email address or name of your co-teacher, and hit **Invite**. The recipient will receive an email inviting them to be a co-teacher of the class.

> **Google Classroom Tip**
>
> It can be great to add a librarian, special-ed teacher, or principal to be a co-teacher to allow them to support your teaching. However, they won't want all of the emails for the class. Direct these co-teachers to use the **Three Lines** menu to go to **Settings**. The last option is **Class Notifications, where** all notifications for an individual class can be disabled.

Google Classroom Updates

Changes and updates will always be a part of Google Classroom.

If you would like to receive updates to this book when changes are made, please subscribe at **alicekeeler.com/gcupdates**.

You can also listen and subscribe to *The Suite Talk* on YouTube or your favorite podcast platform. *The Suite Talk* provides educators with comfortable and simple conversations about new or existing features of Google for Education and practical ideas to implement technology tools in education. You'll find documentation, screencasts, tips, and tricks that help stimulate and engage student learning while making educators work smarter, not harder. Visit **thesuitetalk.com** for more information and subscribe to stay up to date on the latest episodes and content.

One of the best ways to learn Google Classroom is to experience it as a student. Visit **alicekeeler.com/workshops** for a list of interactive workshops using Google Classroom.

Conclusion

Learning can be improved when we use tools like Google Classroom, but only if we start with a mindset focused on interacting with students, improving feedback loops, and applying pedagogy over using tools to allow students to take more control of their learning. Remember: *it is not digital, it is different*. Teaching with technology is a different way of teaching.

We hope this book helps you to get started on your Google Classroom journey. If you would like to learn more about how to teach with Google Apps and Google Classroom check out this free forty-five-minute certification course with Alice Keeler: **screencastify.com/genius**.

Acknowledgements

Thank you to Barton Keeler for your teaching insights and unwavering support.

Thank you to Jim Mattina for your love and support.

Thank you to Sonny Magana: your contributions to education and your enthusiasm are needed. Readers should check out the T3 Framework, a research-based approach to integrating technology, at **bit.ly/T3Academy**.

A special thanks to Peter Leonard for all of your patience, dedication, and assistance while collaborating on edits to this book.

Shout out to the awesome Google Classroom team, who makes writing this book extra hard because they are always making Google Classroom better. It is nice to know that user feedback is considered seriously and that you accommodate educators and students as much as possible. Thank you!

Thank you to Juliette Kuhn, Allison Ermol, and Matt Trammell.

Special thanks to Brittany Mennuti, the former PM for Google Classroom

About the Authors

Alice Keeler

 @alicekeeler

Alice Keeler is a mom of five children and a global leader in educational technology. She has taught high school mathematics since 1999, mostly 1:1, and taught in the teacher-credential program at California State University Fresno. She holds a bachelor's degree in mathematics and a master's degree in educational media design and technology and is a Google Certified Innovator and Google Apps Script Developer. She has worked on projects such as YouTube for Teachers, Google Applied Digital Skills, Google Play for Education, and Bing in the Classroom, and she's the founder of coffeeEDU.

Stepping Up to Google Classroom is the sixth book that Alice has co-authored. Others include *50 Things to Go Further with Google Classroom* and *Ditch That Homework*. She frequently blogs on teaching with G Suite at **alicekeeler.com**.

Kimberly Mattina

 @The_Tech_Lady

Kimberly Mattina is a wife, mother, daughter, educator, and lifelong learner. She has been in education for nearly fifteen years, and is currently a full-time middle school technology teacher and robotics-club advisor in New Jersey. Her motto is #PayitForward.

Kimberly is proud to be a Google for Education Gold Product Expert, Google Cloud Certified–G Suite, a Google Certified Trainer, a Google Certified Educator, a GEG Leader for NJ, an Ozobot and Wakelet Ambassador, and a member of the Computer Science Teachers Association.

In addition to her role as an educator, she is a technology consultant at The Tech Lady, LLC, which provides G Suite for Education training sessions for individuals, small businesses, and school districts. She also provides computer-installation and -repair services. For more information, visit **the-tech-lady.com** or find The Tech Lady on Facebook.

Her passion has led her to create and host *The Suite Talk*, a YouTube show and podcast about helping educators effectively integrate technology into the classroom. It focuses on all things Google and other technology pedagogy and tools for educators. Visit **thesuitetalk.com** for information.

Conferences and Publications

Through the years, Kimberly has presented at many conferences in the tri-state area and edcamps in New Jersey. She's also provided professional development to educators face to face and virtually, focusing on integrating G Suite, Google for Education, and Chromebooks into the classroom.

Her blog, the *Tech Lady*, has been recognized among the top 40 educational technology blogs in 2019 and the top 50 K-12 educational IT blogs in 2018.

She has published several articles, such as "Three Technology Tools to Engage Students with the 5 Cs of Education" for learning.com, "What's in Your Tech Toolbox" for NJEA Review, "A Framework for Educators: Leveraging Free Social Media to Brand and Communicate" for NJPSA, and she's written blog posts for Screencastify, Ozobot, and Wakelet.

More from Dave Burgess Consulting, Inc.

Since 2012, DBCI has been publishing books that inspire and equip educators to be their best. For more information on our titles or to purchase bulk orders for your school, district, or book study, visit **DaveBurgessConsulting.com/DBCIbooks**.

More Teaching Methods & Materials

All 4s and 5s by Andrew Sharos

Boredom Busters by Katie Powell

The Classroom Chef by John Stevens and Matt Vaudrey

The Collaborative Classroom by Trevor Muir

Copyrighteous by Diana Gill

Ditch That Homework by Matt Miller and Alice Keeler

Ditch That Textbook by Matt Miller

Don't Ditch That Tech by Matt Miller, Nate Ridgway, and Angelia Ridgway

EDrenaline Rush by John Meehan

Educated by Design by Michael Cohen, The Tech Rabbi

The EduProtocol Field Guide by Marlena Hebern and Jon Corippo

The EduProtocol Field Guide: Book 2 by Marlena Hebern and Jon Corippo

Instant Relevance by Denis Sheeran

LAUNCH by John Spencer and A.J. Juliani

Make Learning MAGICAL by Tisha Richmond

Pure Genius by Don Wettrick

The Revolution by Darren Ellwein and Derek McCoy

Shift This! by Joy Kirr

Skyrocket Your Teacher Coaching by Michael Cary Sonbert

Spark Learning by Ramsey Musallam

Sparks in the Dark by Travis Crowder and Todd Nesloney

Table Talk Math by John Stevens

The Wild Card by Hope and Wade King

The Writing on the Classroom Wall by Steve Wyborney

Like a PIRATE™ Series

Teach Like a PIRATE by Dave Burgess

eXPlore Like a Pirate by Michael Matera

Learn Like a Pirate by Paul Solarz

Play Like a Pirate by Quinn Rollins

Run Like a Pirate by Adam Welcome

Lead Like a PIRATE™ Series

Lead Like a PIRATE by Shelley Burgess and Beth Houf

Balance Like a Pirate by Jessica Cabeen, Jessica Johnson, and Sarah Johnson

Lead beyond Your Title by Nili Bartley

Lead with Appreciation by Amber Teamann and Melinda Miller

Lead with Culture by Jay Billy

Lead with Instructional Rounds by Vicki Wilson

Lead with Literacy by Mandy Ellis

Leadership & School Culture

Culturize by Jimmy Casas

Escaping the School Leader's Dunk Tank by Rebecca Coda and Rick Jetter

From Teacher to Leader by Starr Sackstein

The Innovator's Mindset by George Couros

It's OK to Say "They" by Christy Whittlesey

Kids Deserve It! by Todd Nesloney and Adam Welcome

Live Your Excellence by Jimmy Casas

Let Them Speak by Rebecca Coda and Rick Jetter

The Limitless School by Abe Hege and Adam Dovico

Next-Level Teaching by Jonathan Alsheimer

The Pepper Effect by Sean Gaillard

The Principled Principal by Jeffrey Zoul and Anthony McConnell

Relentless by Hamish Brewer

The Secret Solution by Todd Whitaker, Sam Miller, and Ryan Donlan

Start. Right. Now. by Todd Whitaker, Jeffrey Zoul, and Jimmy Casas

Stop. Right. Now. by Jimmy Casas and Jeffrey Zoul

They Call Me "Mr. De" by Frank DeAngelis

Unmapped Potential by Julie Hasson and Missy Lennard

Word Shift by Joy Kirr

Your School Rocks by Ryan McLane and Eric Lowe

Technology & Tools

50 Things You Can Do with Google Classroom by Alice Keeler and Libbi Miller

50 Things to Go Further with Google Classroom by Alice Keeler and Libbi Miller

140 Twitter Tips for Educators by Brad Currie, Billy Krakower, and Scott Rocco

Block Breaker by Brian Aspinall

Code Breaker by Brian Aspinall

Google Apps for Littles by Christine Pinto and Alice Keeler

Master the Media by Julie Smith

Reality Bytes by Christine Lion-Bailey, Jesse Lubinsky, and Micah Shippee, PhD

Shake Up Learning by Kasey Bell

Social LEADia by Jennifer Casa-Todd

Teaching Math with Google Apps by Alice Keeler and Diana Herrington

Teachingland by Amanda Fox and Mary Ellen Weeks

Inspiration, Professional Growth & Personal Development

Be REAL by Tara Martin

Be the One for Kids by Ryan Sheehy

The Coach ADVenture by Amy Illingworth

Creatively Productive by Lisa Johnson

Educational Eye Exam by Alicia Ray

The EduNinja Mindset by Jennifer Burdis

Empower Our Girls by Lynmara Colón and
Adam Welcome

Finding Lifelines by Andrew Grieve and
Andrew Sharos

The Four O'Clock Faculty by Rich Czyz

How Much Water Do We Have? by Pete and
Kris Nunweiler

P Is for Pirate by Dave and Shelley Burgess

A Passion for Kindness by Tamara Letter

The Path to Serendipity by Allyson Apsey

Sanctuaries by Dan Tricarico

The SECRET SAUCE by Rich Czyz

Shattering the Perfect Teacher Myth by Aaron Hogan

Stories from Webb by Todd Nesloney

Talk to Me by Kim Bearden

Teach Better by Chad Ostrowski, Tiffany Ott, Rae
Hughart, and Jeff Gargas

Teach Me, Teacher by Jacob Chastain

TeamMakers by Laura Robb and Evan Robb

Through the Lens of Serendipity by Allyson Apsey

The Zen Teacher by Dan Tricarico

Children's Books

Beyond Us by Aaron Polansky

Cannonball In by Tara Martin

Dolphins in Trees by Aaron Polansky

I Want to Be a Lot by Ashley Savage

The Princes of Serendip by Allyson Apsey

The Wild Card Kids by Hope and Wade King

Zom-Be a Design Thinker by Amanda Fox

Made in the USA
Middletown, DE
31 August 2020